SUPER
Things to Do
After School

Written by Beth Kneeland Pickett
Additional material written by Joanna Siebert

Illustrated by Eric Angeloch
Additional illustrations by Neal Yamamoto

LOWELL HOUSE JUVENILE

LOS ANGELES

NTC/Contemporary Publishing Group

NOTE: The numbered squiggle in the upper right-hand corner of each activity indicates the level of difficulty, with 1 as the easiest and 3 as the hardest.

Managing Director and Publisher: Jack Artenstein
Director of Publishing Services: Rena Copperman
Editorial Director, Juvenile: Brenda Pope-Ostrow
Director of Juvenile Development: Amy Downing
Director of Art Production: Bret Perry
Project Editor: Joanna Siebert
Cover Photo: Ann Bogart

Library of Congress Catalog Card Number: 98-66658
ISBN: 1-56565-686-5

Lowell House books can be purchased at special discounts
when ordered in bulk for premiums and special sales.
Contact Customer Service at:
NTC/Contemporary Publishing Group, Inc.
4255 West Touhy Avenue, Lincolnwood (Chicago), Illinois 60646-1975 U.S.A.
1-800-323-4900

Printed and bound in the United States of America

10 9 8 7 6 5 4 3 2 1

CONTENTS

· ·

SCHOOL'S OUT!

Rrrrinngg! There goes the bell—school's out! Now what do you do?

After school is the perfect time to try new things. It's an opportunity to be creative and to explore different interests. Whether you are hanging out with friends or on your own, *50 Nifty Super Things to Do After School* has tons of great activities to choose from—and plenty of things to keep you busy!

You can read this book from beginning to end, or simply flip through and choose an activity that appeals to you. At the back of the book you'll find a quick reference list to help you choose the perfect project for different situations. If you don't have many supplies around the house, take a look at "Make Your Own Materials." This section is filled with ideas on how you can adapt these projects to use materials you already have.

If you get the munchies after school (and who doesn't?), try the easy-to-make recipes in this book. These simple snacks are especially cool because you can change them depending on the ingredients you have and the types of food you like.

BEFORE YOU BEGIN

When you select an activity, keep these guidelines in mind:

• Parental supervision is recommended or required for a few of the activities. Make sure a parent or another adult is available to help if you choose to do one of those activities.

• The difficulty of each activity varies. Check the number marked in the upper right-hand corner for the level of difficulty.

• Think about the amount of time you will need to complete the project. Be sure to include plenty of time for cleanup!

• Find a good place to do each activity. If you think the project will be messy, try to do it outdoors or in a garage, or find someplace that is easy to clean up, such as a table or an uncarpeted floor. Put down newspaper or cardboard, and wear old clothes when necessary.

• Make sure that you have all the supplies you will need, or a reasonable substitute, before you begin. If you need to borrow any materials from a parent or a sibling, be sure to ask permission ahead of time.

• Read all the directions carefully before you begin to work on a project.

AFTER-SCHOOL TIP #1

Create a system to keep track of your homework assignments. This will help you juggle your time and remember exactly what you need to turn in to the teacher each day. With the system below, all you need is a blank piece of paper or a notebook. Make a grid like the one you see here, or develop your own system.

Date Assigned	Subject	Assignment	Date Due	Done

SMART SNACKS

Eating a healthy snack when you get home from school will give you energy to enjoy the rest of the day. Snack time can be as simple or as creative as you want it to be. Try experimenting with a new recipe, or stick with an old favorite if you're in a rush. Here are a few simple snack ideas that you can make in a snap. (If you want to make a snack to share with a friend, just double the recipe.)

FRUIT SMOOTHIE

Perfect for a refreshing pick-me-up!

- lowfat vanilla yogurt
- ice
- orange juice
- any of the following: bananas, strawberries, watermelon, blueberries, oranges, peaches, pineapple, raspberries, or other fruit

In a blender, mix approximately 1 cup yogurt, 1 cup ice, and 1 cup orange juice with any fruit you like. Make flavorful smoothies by mixing different kinds of fruit each time.

CHEESE STIX

A tasty twist on pretzel sticks

- nacho cheese sauce or Cheez Whiz®
- pretzel sticks

Pour some cheese sauce into a small bowl. Heat in a microwave, according to the directions on the jar or container of cheese. Dip pretzel sticks into the sauce and eat.

> ### AFTER-SCHOOL TIP #2
> If you can, do your chores as soon as you get home from school. Then you can enjoy whatever free time you have left! (And it will keep your parents happy.)

POPCORN WITH PIZZAZZ

Spice up an old standby!

- one bag of plain microwave popcorn
- nonstick vegetable spray
- one of the following: parmesan cheese, chili pepper, grated cheese, taco seasoning, ranch-style dressing mix

Follow the directions on the bag to prepare plain microwave popcorn, then pour the popcorn into a bowl. Lightly coat the popcorn with the nonstick vegetable spray. Sprinkle the popcorn with one of the seasonings listed above or anything else that sounds tasty to you. Mix the popcorn with your hands and eat.

POWER CRACKERS

Packed with protein for extra energy

- crackers
- any of the following combinations: meat and cheese, peanut butter and jelly, cream cheese and olives

Create mini sandwiches with any kind of cracker you like. Try any of the exciting combinations listed above or create your own. Simply stack the ingredients between two crackers.

AFTER-SCHOOL TIP #3

Set aside a regular study time. Whether you prefer to study in the afternoon or in the evening, a routine will make it easier to concentrate on the books. If you finish your homework right after school, you'll be able to enjoy the rest of the evening. However, if clubs or other activities keep you busy in the afternoon, doing your homework after dinner will be easier. Be sure to allow yourself enough time to finish before you get too tired.

CINNAMON TOAST

A simply super sweet treat

- whole wheat bread
- butter
- cinnamon
- sugar

Toast a piece of bread. Spread a light coat of butter over the bread. In a small cup, mix 1 tablespoon sugar with ¼ teaspoon cinnamon. Sprinkle some of the cinnamon sugar mixture over the bread.

FRUIT BITES

So yummy, you won't realize how healthy it is!

- any of the following: grapes, cherries, blueberries, melon, oranges, peaches, pineapple, raspberries, strawberries, or other fruit
- one dressing: strawberry or lemon yogurt; ½ cup plain yogurt mixed with peanut butter and honey to taste; applesauce with a trace of cinnamon

Wash the fruit and cut it into bite-sized pieces. Arrange the pieces on a plate. Mix one of the dressings listed above in a small bowl. Use a toothpick to spear pieces of fruit and dip them into the dressing. You can jazz up this recipe by freezing the fruit pieces first—it makes the perfect snack for a warm spring afternoon!

> ### AFTER-SCHOOL TIP #4
> Create your own study space. Choose a place to study that is quiet and well lit. Try to avoid distractions, such as a television. Use a desk or a table where you can spread out your books, and always sit on a comfortable chair.

PINWHEELS

Wait till you wrap your fingers around this one!

- tortilla or lavash
- whipped cream cheese
- turkey
- shredded carrots
- sliced olives
- alfalfa sprouts

Lay a tortilla on a plate. Spread a spoonful of whipped cream cheese over the tortilla, then top with a slice of turkey, shredded carrots, sliced olives, and alfalfa sprouts. Roll the tortilla tightly, then cut into 2-inch-thick slices.

JUICE CUPS

A delicious homemade slushy

- any flavored juice

Pour some juice into a small paper cup, about two-thirds full. Carefully place the cup in the freezer. After half an hour, the juice should be slushy. After one to two hours, the juice should be frozen solid. You can push your slushy out of the cup or use a spoon to scoop it out.

AFTER-SCHOOL TIP #5

Have you ever heard of a "thinking cap"? Wear a baseball cap, a bandanna, or even a funny headband when you study to help you concentrate. There's nothing like a thinking cap to keep your mind on the books! If you wear your special hat every time you study, and only when you study, it will become an essential part of your study routine. It will also show others that you don't want to be disturbed unless it's important.

ANTS ON A LOG

A creepy-crawly classic

- celery
- peanut butter
- raisins

Cut a celery stalk into 2-inch-long pieces. Spread peanut butter inside the celery, then top with raisins.

BANANA SANDWICH

An intriguing taste sensation

- two graham crackers
- one banana
- honey

Break each graham cracker in half, then arrange two pieces on a plate. Mash the banana in a small bowl, then mix in ¼ teaspoon honey. If you want to make it sweeter, add up to 1 teaspoon honey; if you don't want it to be sweet, skip the honey altogether. Spread the mixture over the graham cracker pieces on the plate. Place the remaining graham cracker pieces on top of each to make two sandwiches.

AFTER-SCHOOL TIP #6

Organize a study group. Since the key word is *study*, choose a friend or two who you know you will be able to study with. You'll probably feel more motivated to study when you are with someone else who is hard at work. Just encourage each other to get your homework done, so that you can have fun together later!

COTTAGE CHEESE DELIGHT

A cool surprise (and healthy, too)

- cottage cheese
- pineapple chunks
- maraschino cherry

Spoon cottage cheese into a small bowl. Add pineapple chunks to the cottage cheese, and top with a maraschino cherry.

MINI PIZZAS

A mini meal

- one English muffin, sliced in half
- pizza sauce or tomato sauce
- any shredded cheese:
  mozzarella, parmesan,
  cheddar
- pepperoni
- olives
- onions
- green peppers

Separate the English muffin into halves, and arrange them ragged side up on a microwave-safe plate (or on tinfoil if you are using a toaster oven). Spoon a thin layer of pizza sauce or tomato sauce on each half. Sprinkle cheese on top. Add pepperoni, olives, onions, green peppers, or whatever you'd like. Heat in the microwave or a toaster oven until cheese is melted.

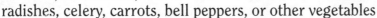

CRUNCHY BITS

Crunch, crunch, crunch—this one is a handful!

• banana or apple
• peanut butter
• granola or cornflakes

Cut a banana or apple into quarters, so that the pieces are manageable. Cover each piece of fruit with a thin layer of peanut butter. Spread granola or cornflakes on a plate. Roll fruit over granola or cornflakes until coated.

VEGGIES GALORE

Finger food fun!

• packet of ranch-style dressing mix
• sour cream
• any of the following: cherry tomatoes, broccoli, cauliflower, radishes, celery, carrots, bell peppers, or other vegetables

In the container or a small bowl, mix the entire packet of ranch dressing with 2 cups sour cream. Wash the vegetables and cut into small pieces. Dip veggies and eat.

AFTER-SCHOOL TIP #7

Make a set of flashcards to help you learn facts on almost any subject. All you need is a pack of index cards (or paper cut into 3" wide by 5" long rectangles). Write a math problem, science term, or vocabulary word on one side of a card, then write the answer or definition on the other side. You'll get some practice just by making the cards. You can test yourself by reading each card and answering aloud before you check the other side. Or you may want to have a friend or a family member quiz you.

MAKE YOUR OWN MATERIALS

Just because you don't have everything listed for one of the projects in this book doesn't mean you have to miss out! As long as you're creative and flexible, you can enjoy every activity. Simply adapt the project to work using what you have. You will probably discover ways to substitute materials on your own, but here are a few ideas to help you get started.

For many crafts, you can try these substitutions:

- use tape instead of glue, or vice versa
- use a cut-up brown paper bag, or poster board, instead of construction paper
- use a clock or a watch with a second hand instead of a kitchen timer
- use rectangles of paper, preferably white construction paper or poster board, instead of index cards

> ### AFTER-SCHOOL TIP #8
> As you try different projects, think about the ones that you enjoy the most. You may discover that you have a particular interest in science or in helping others. After school is a great time to try out a new hobby or practice a special talent.

GYOTAKU (page 18): If there's not a fish to be found, try this project with other materials that will make an interesting imprint, such as a leaf or tree bark. You could even try the bottom of an old tennis shoe.

INDOOR TABLE HOCKEY (page 25): If you don't have your own Pogs® for a start-up game of Indoor Table Hockey, you can make a set. Find a piece of thin cardboard that is at least 8″ wide by 12″ long, or use smaller pieces of cardboard. Trace the circle on this page onto a plain white piece of paper. Cut the circle out, then use it as a guide to trace 24 circles onto the cardboard. Carefully cut out the circles. If you want to, you can decorate your new game pieces with colorful markers.

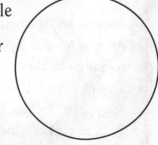

ROBIN HOOD HAT (page 30): If you don't have green felt, try another type of stiff fabric, or even green construction paper, to make the hat.

FOOT VOLLEYBALL (page 31): If you don't have any stakes to attach the rope to, tie the rope between two trees or poles, about 10 inches above the ground. If you don't have a sheet to use as a net, spread pages of newspaper over the line, then staple the bottom edges together so that the newspaper won't blow off.

BELLS IN THE WIND (page 36): Use a coat hanger if you don't have an unsharpened pencil to hang the bells from.

FIVE-TOE PICKUP (page 37): Instead of pie tins, use paper plates as the goal markers.

A WHALE OF A SECRET! (page 45): Use an extra-large bowl, or even the sink, instead of a bucket to hold the water.

WINDSOCK WONDER (page 52): If you don't have an oatmeal container, take a large piece of lightweight cardboard (approximately 12″ by 12″), bend it into a cylinder shape, then staple the edges together. Also, if you don't have seven pieces of fabric to hang on the bottom of the windsock, try using cellophane or ribbon.

STAINED "GLASS" MOBILE (page 56): If you don't have fishing line for the mobile, use thin string.

THE SUNNY DAY RAIN STICK (page 60): Try making this instrument with tiny pebbles, dried beans, or sunflower seeds in their shells if you don't have any split peas.

AFTER-SCHOOL TIP #9

Think of each activity as a stepping stone to many more fun projects. The possibilities are endless—you can research subjects that interest you, write stories, or try other forms of art. Here's one idea: After you make the Robin Hood Hat on page 30, look around your home and find other props you can use to complete the costume. Write a play about Robin Hood's adventures, and enlist a few friends to help you act it out. Send invitations to all of your friends and family, then perform your masterpiece. What other ideas can you come up with to create more fun?

MAGAZINE MEDLEY

There are approximately 6 billion people on Earth, but there's only one you! Show your true colors with this cool collage.

WHAT YOU'LL NEED

- old magazines
- scissors
- pictures of yourself, your family, and your friends
- construction paper
- glue

DIRECTIONS

1 Make sure it's all right with your parents for you to cut up old magazines. Then go through them and cut out pictures of activities you like and words or phrases that describe you. Also, ask permission to cut out and use pictures of yourself, your family, and your friends.

2 Arrange the cutouts on a large piece of construction paper, then glue them down. You can hang your collage in your room to remind yourself of what an awesome individual you are.

FURTHER FUN

Make a collage for a friend, using words or phrases that describe him or her. It's a thoughtful gift that you will enjoy making.

DINOSAUR TAG

Tyrannosaurus, Brontosaurus, Stegosaurus, oh, my!

WHAT YOU'LL NEED

- four or more players
- open, grassy area
- five dinosaur names (such as Stegosaurus, Triceratops, Tyrannosaurus, Brontosaurus, and Seismosaurus)
- pencil
- paper

DIRECTIONS

1 Pick someone to be the King Dinosaur. The King Dinosaur picks one dinosaur name from the list of five, then writes it down on a piece of paper and puts the paper in his or her pocket.

2 The King Dinosaur closes his or her eyes and counts to ten, then is free to try to tag any of the other players. When the King Dinosaur tags another player, the tagged player must whisper one of the five dinosaur names into the King Dinosaur's ear. None of the other players should hear what is whispered.

3 If the name the player whispers *matches* the name that the King Dinosaur has picked, that player becomes a member of the King's court. Then he or she must help the King chase and tag the others.

4 If the name the player whispers *does not match* the name that the King Dinosaur has written on the paper, that player is set free. That player must guess a different dinosaur name from the list each time he or she is tagged by the King or a member of the King's court.

5 When a member of the King's court tags another player, the tagged person whispers a dinosaur name in the court member's ear. Again, if the dinosaur name matches the name that is in the King's pocket, then the person who is tagged must join the King's court. Continue tagging and "appointing" people to the court until all but one player are in the King's court.

6 The last free player becomes the new King Dinosaur. That person picks a new dinosaur name, writes it down, puts it in his or her pocket, and the game starts over.

GYOTAKU

PARENTAL SUPERVISION RECOMMENDED

Asian fishermen started *gyotaku* (fish printing) to prove the size of their catch to trade in the market. Now fish printing is used as decoration and for a somewhat slimy dose of good fun.

WHAT YOU'LL NEED

- old clothes or a smock
- newspaper
- whole, very fresh fish (flat fish with lots of scales, such as perch and flounder, work best)
- paper towel

- modeling clay
- medium-sized paintbrush
- water-based, nontoxic paints
- sketch paper
- tiny paintbrush

DIRECTIONS

❶ Put on some old clothes or a smock and cover your work space—both the table and floor—with newspaper.

❷ Wash the fish thoroughly with water and a touch of soap to remove any slimy mucus. Be gentle so that you don't loosen the scales or damage the fins. Dry the fish with a paper towel and lay it on the newspaper that's covering your work table.

❸ The fins will probably be folded down. Fan them open, then tuck the modeling clay underneath the fish's fins to keep them open.

clay

❹ Using the medium-sized paintbrush, coat the fish's body and fins (but not the eye!) with two thin layers of paint. Put on the first coat by moving your brush in long strokes from the fish's head to its tail. Put on the second coat by running the brush again in long strokes from the tail back to the head.

❺ Place your sketch paper gently over the fish and press. Make sure to press the paper against all the different parts

18

of the fish, especially the fins. Because the fish is round and the paper is flat, you may need to gently roll the paper around the fish in sections, so that the paper doesn't wrinkle.

6 Peel off the paper and take a look at your fish print. Note any changes you'll want to make on the next print. Set the print in a safe place to dry. Then repaint the fish to make another print (wash the fish again if you're going to use a new color). You can keep making prints as long as the fish's scales and fins hold together—usually about three to ten prints, depending on the individual fish.

7 When your prints are dry, use the tiny paintbrush and a different color paint to fill in the fish's eye. Add any other details.

8 Wash the fish very thoroughly until all visible signs of the paint are removed. If you wish, ask an adult to fillet the fish, but be sure to remove the skin, head, tail, and any other parts that came in contact with the paint. Enjoy!

FURTHER FUN

If you'd rather not work with an animal, try printing with plants or plant parts such as leaves and branches. Because these objects are very light, you may need to flatten some clay into a disk shape, then press your object into the clay before you paint and print it.

COLOR ME SLIMY

Cornstarch and water make a freaky substance that is totally *thixotropic*! (It acts like a solid and a liquid at the same time.)

WHAT YOU'LL NEED

- ½ cup cornstarch
- 6 tablespoons water
- large mixing bowl
- mixing spoon

- newspaper
- four small bowls
- food coloring (any four colors)
- white construction paper

DIRECTIONS

1 Combine the cornstarch with 4 tablespoons water in the large mixing bowl and stir until well mixed. Pick up a glob and place it in the palm of your hand. It should slowly flow into a pool of liquid. Now make a fist around it and squeeze it into a ball shape. It should hold the shape for a few seconds, then "melt" into a liquid again. If it's too crumbly, add a few more drops of water.

2 When you're done watching it change forms, put the cornstarch ball back into the mixing bowl and mix in 2 tablespoons water. It should act like a liquid now.

3 Lay down the newspaper to cover your work area. Divide the liquid into four small bowls. Use food coloring (about 2 to 3 drops) to make a different color cornstarch mixture in each bowl.

4 Lay out your construction paper. Dip your fingers into the bowls and fingerpaint with the cornstarch mixtures to make a masterpiece of color and imagination.

CHICKEN NOISEMAKER

There's a chicken loose in the house! Or is it just an *audio* illusion?

WHAT YOU'LL NEED

- ballpoint pen
- plastic cup
- 14-inch piece of cotton string
- two safety pins
- piece of kitchen sponge, 1 inch wide by 2 inches long
- 12-inch piece of dental floss

DIRECTIONS

1 Use the writing end of the pen to poke a hole in the very center of the bottom of the cup. The hole should be just big enough to allow the string to pass through it.

2 Thread half the length of the string through the cup. Tie a safety pin to each end of the string. The safety pins will keep the string from being pulled all the way through the hole. Hold the cup upright and pull the string down.

3 Dampen the sponge piece and fold it around the string. Use the dental floss to tie the sponge tightly around the string.

4 Moisten the string under a faucet. Slide the sponge to the top of the string. Now hold the cup in one hand and the sponge in the other.

5 Squeeze the sponge as you pull it with quick, jerky motions, down the length of the string. Listen to your chicken cluck, cluck, cluck.

6 SCHOOL-YEAR REMEMBRANCE ALBUM

Preserve your memories of friends and fun in this keepsake you'll treasure for years.

WHAT YOU'LL NEED

- scissors
- construction paper
- hole punch
- three 10-inch pieces of yarn

- pen or colored markers
- glue
- school pictures of yourself and friends

DIRECTIONS

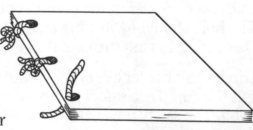

1 To create this special album, start by cutting out ten pieces of construction paper, each 7 inches wide by 10 inches tall. Using the hole punch, punch three holes along the left side of all the pieces of the construction paper (make sure all the holes line up). Thread a piece of yarn through each hole and gently tie it off. Don't tie it too tight or the pages of your album won't turn.

2 Start the album by introducing yourself. Write "Me" at the top of the page, then fill in the rest of the page with your name, any nicknames your friends call you, your teacher's name, your grade, and the name of your school. Glue a picture of yourself on the page.

3 Write the word "Friends" on the top of the next page. Glue school pictures of your friends onto the page, and write each friend's name under his or her photo. Also write in the names of friends whose pictures you don't have. The "Friends" section may take up more than one page.

4 Write "What's Hot?" on the next page. Fill in the name of your favorite band, your favorite movie from this year, and any fads that are currently taking over your school.

5 Write "Cool Stuff I Do" on the next page. List all the things you do at recess or after school. List your favorite sports and activities. Glue in either a photo or drawing of yourself playing a sport or enjoying a hobby.

6 Fill the other pages with items to help you remember the school year. You can glue in movie ticket stubs or report cards. Write about things that have happened to you or about activities with which you are involved. What are the best and the worst things that happened to you so far this year? If you're still at the beginning of the school year, keep five or six pages blank so you can add things as the year goes by.

7 You don't have to finish the album in one day. Once a week, you could take a few minutes after school to add new things. By the end of the school year, you'll have lots of good memories about the year's activities. Then put your album in a safe place so it will keep forever!

FURTHER FUN

A school-year remembrance album makes a great gift for a friend or classmate. Be sure to list his or her teacher, other friends, pets, the activities he or she enjoys, what you like most about him or her—anything that will make it special for him or her. Also include blank pages that he or she can fill in.

FASHIONABLE FIDO

It's time for the aCATemy awards! Spend an afternoon with your favorite cat or dog (or stuffed animal) to create a furry version of your favorite movie star, rock star, or fictional movie character.

WHAT YOU'LL NEED

- old clothes and accessories (with a parent's permission)
- cooperative dog or cat, or a stuffed animal
- instant camera with film (optional)

DIRECTIONS

❶ Before you begin your clothes hunt, think of the character that you'd like your animal to imitate. You'll probably need to find a hat, shoes, socks, a shirt or sweater or short dress, sunglasses, a wig—anything you can find that will help you transform your four-legged friend into a celebrity. Find clothes that will help you create the right image. For example, a Western look would include a cowboy hat, boots, and bandanna. A glamorous look could include a feathered boa, a big wig, and sunglasses.

❷ Think of a funny name for your new celebrity. If you're transforming your cat into Julia Roberts, you can name it Julieeeeeow Roberts. A basketball-playing dog could be Charles *Bark*ley.

❸ Once you've gathered the clothes and accessories you'll need, and have decided on a funny name, have your pet (or stuffed animal) sit in front of you. Gently put the clothes and accessories on the animal. Don't put anything on your animal that might harm it or make it feel uncomfortable.

❹ When you're finished, invite friends or family members over to introduce them to your new celebrity. If you have a camera, have the big star's "fans" pose with it for a picture!

INDOOR TABLE HOCKEY

This game puts a new spin on Pogs®.

WHAT YOU'LL NEED

• two players   • flat, smooth table   • twenty-four Pogs

DIRECTIONS

1 The object of this game is to be the first player to get rid of all your Pogs. Players should face each other on opposite ends of the table. Each player starts with twelve Pogs and should divide them into two stacks of six each. The stacks should be placed approximately 6 inches apart. These are the goalposts for your game of hockey.

2 To play, the first player takes a Pog from one of his or her columns. The player places the Pog flat on the table, then shoots the Pog from behind his or her goalposts using a quick flick of the fingers. The Pog should skim across the table. If the player flicks his Pog *between* the other player's goalposts, the other player must put the Pog on one of his or her stacks. If the first player doesn't make it through the other player's goalposts, then he or she must keep the Pog. Players take turns whether or not the goal was successful.

3 The game is almost over when a player is down to one Pog. Because he or she has too few Pogs to form goalposts, the other player must try to flick a Pog so that it hits the player's last Pog. If it hits, the player with one Pog must keep the other player's Pog. If it doesn't hit, the one-Pog player gets another chance to shoot. If the one-Pog player flicks his or her last Pog between the other player's goalposts, he or she wins the game.

25

RAIN READER

It's raining, it's pouring. How much rain is falling? Your rain reader will tell you. And if it's not raining, you can still create your rain gauge to be prepared to catch every raindrop when the next storm comes!

WHAT YOU'LL NEED

- large, empty glass jar (mayonnaise jars work well)
- funnel that fits the mouth of the glass jar
- masking tape
- kitchen timer with buzzer
- ruler

DIRECTIONS

1 Clean out the glass jar and remove any labels still stuck to it. Place the funnel snugly in the mouth of the jar and tape it in place (see illustration).

2 If it's already raining outside, you're in luck. Set the kitchen timer for two hours. Then go outside and set the rain reader down in an open flat area, where trees or roofs won't interfere with the falling rain. Come back inside and get dry!

3 When the kitchen buzzer goes off, retrieve your rain reader. Put it on a table and hold the ruler up to the jar so you can measure how much rain has fallen. Divide that number by two and you'll know how much rain has fallen per hour over the last two hours. If it's only raining lightly, you'll want to leave it out for a few more hours—long enough for a measurable amount of rain to fall. To find out how much rain has fallen per hour, divide the amount of rain by the number of hours you left the rain reader outside.

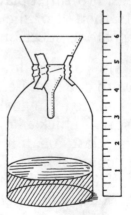

4 Listen to the evening news or read the next day's paper to find out how your measurements compare to the measurements given by professional weather reporters.

 **COLORFUL CREATURE CREATIONS**

Snip, clip, shuffle, pick! It's a race against the clock—and each other—to see who has the quickest eyes and fastest hands.

WHAT YOU'LL NEED

- three or more players
- several sheets of construction paper in different colors
- scissors
- clock or watch with second hand

DIRECTIONS

1 Have each player cut ten squares, ten circles, ten triangles, and ten rectangles of different colors and sizes from the construction paper. Have all the players sit in a circle and put all the cut-out shapes into a pile in the center of the circle. Mix them up.

2 Assign one player to be the timer. The remaining players are shape-makers. The timer chooses a type of animal and tells the shape-makers to make that animal out of the pieces of construction paper. Then the timer tells the shape-makers to "Go!" and begins timing on the clock or watch.

3 After sixty seconds, the timer says "Stop!" The timer looks at the animals created by each shape-maker, then decides whose animal has the best likeness to the animal he or she named.

4 The person who made the best animal is the winner and becomes the timer for the next round.

5 To make the game easier or harder, adjust the amount of time that the shape-makers have to make their animals.

FLYING DISK CROQUET

A bit of practice and a quick flick of the wrist is the secret to being a champion at this game.

WHAT YOU'LL NEED

- two or more players
- four old wire hangers
- open grassy area
- pen
- four pieces of paper
- flat plastic can lid (such as a coffee can lid) for each player

DIRECTIONS

1 Take apart the hangers by untwisting the wrapped wire at the neck of the hanger. Bend each hanger into a *U* shape (wires are hard to bend—don't worry if your shapes are a bit crooked). Ends should be about 12 inches apart. Take the hangers outside to a grassy area where you can set up and play the game. The hangers will be the goalposts.

2 Decide where you want the goalposts to be. A simple course could be set up like a baseball diamond, with one goalpost in each of four corners. Another sample pattern might be like the one shown here (see illustration).

3 To set up a goalpost, grab a wire hanger by both ends and push the ends deep into the grass. Make sure the ends are pushed in deep enough so they won't come out easily, but not so deep that there's no room for a disk to fly through the goalpost. Add more goalposts or put the goalposts farther apart to make the course more challenging.

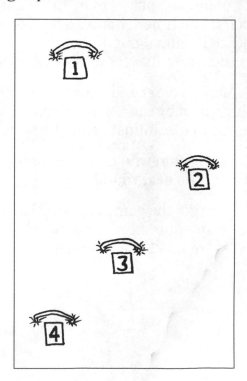

4 Write one number, from 1 to 4, on each piece of paper. Place one numbered piece of paper in front of each goalpost. The numbers on the paper determine which goalpost the players must get through first, second, and so on. Now the course is ready for play.

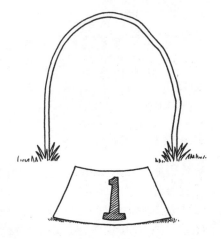

5 Each player lines up about 8 feet behind the first goalpost. The first player tries to get his or her disk through the first goalpost by tossing it. If he or she misses, the next player's turn begins. When a player successfully tosses his or her disk through the first goalpost, he or she goes to the spot where the disk landed, stands on that spot, and tries to toss the disk through the next goalpost. The player's turn ends when the disk doesn't make it through the goalpost.

6 The first player to toss his or her disk through every goalpost is the winner.

FURTHER FUN

Have a neighborhood disk croquet challenge. Set up the game to run from one house to another, in yards where you have permission to put the goalposts. You'll probably need to make at least six additional posts.

ROBIN HOOD HAT

Hi ho! This merry hat will get you in the spirit for adventure!

WHAT YOU'LL NEED

- piece of green felt, 12 inches wide by 14 inches long
- stapler   • glue
- ribbons, feathers, buttons, colored felt-tipped pens, and/or glitter

DIRECTIONS

❶ Place the piece of felt flat in front of you. Fold the felt in half so the top edge meets the bottom edge. Fold the upper right- and left-hand corners in toward the center (see illustration).

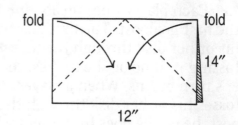

❷ Fold the bottom flap up as shown, and staple it in place. Turn the hat over, and fold the remaining flap up, stapling it in place as well. Voilà! You've made a green felt hat just like Robin Hood used to wear.

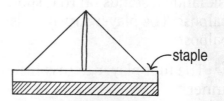

❸ Decorate your hat by gluing on ribbons, feathers, buttons, or any other objects that you'd like to use. Draw colorful designs with your pens, or add some glitter. Wear your wonderful hat as you wander the house in search of further after-school adventures.

FOOT VOLLEYBALL

You'll get a real kick out of this game, which is a variation of a sport played in Thailand. The object is to pass a ball back and forth over a net using only your knees or feet—no hands allowed!

WHAT YOU'LL NEED

- two or more players
- soft, grassy area
- rubber mallet
- two 12-inch or longer sturdy wooden stakes
- 10-foot length of rope
- old twin-sized sheet (get permission from an adult before you use it!)
- volleyball or soccer ball

DIRECTIONS

1 Find a soft, grassy area. Use the rubber mallet to hammer the stakes into the ground. The stakes should be placed about 7 feet apart. Tie one end of the rope around one stake, then run the rest of the rope over to the other stake and tie the end so the rope stretches tightly between the stakes. Drape the sheet lengthwise over the rope. This will be your net.

2 Now you're ready to play! Divide the players into equal numbers (or as close to equal numbers as possible) on both sides of the net, then toss the ball in the air to begin. See how many times the players can pass the ball back and forth over the net using only their knees or feet.

3 To start, allow the ball to bounce once or twice before sending it back over the net. When you get really good, try to get it back and forth over the net without letting it bounce at all. Have the players count out loud each time the ball goes over the net. If someone touches the ball with a hand or head, or if it rolls away from the playing area, the counting must begin all over again. The goal is to set your own record for the number of times the ball goes over the net. Then beat *that* record!

 # 14 PINE NEEDLE SPACE BOOTS

PARENTAL SUPERVISION RECOMMENDED

Astronauts wear thick, padded boots attached to their space suits when they bounce along the moon's surface. You can make your own pair of space boots without even leaving Earth!

WHAT YOU'LL NEED

- scissors   • pair of old panty hose
- old pants and shoes (hiking boots work best)
- four shoe boxes full of brown pine needles
  (brown, fallen leaves or palm fronds work well, too)
- roll of silver duct tape

DIRECTIONS

❶ Use the scissors to cut the legs off the panty hose, making the cut at knee level. Save the two leggings and throw the rest away. Put on old pants and shoes, then go outside to make your boots.

❷ Put on one of the panty hose leggings over your right shoe, and pull it up over your jeans until it reaches your knee. Take your pine needles (or other dry plant material) and shove them down to the bottom of the panty hose. Pack the pine needles all around your shoe (even under your shoe). Keep packing the plant material into the panty hose until you have a 1-inch-thick layer of padding all around your leg.

❸ Now follow the same procedure for your other leg.

❹ Finally, one leg at a time, wrap a layer of duct tape all around the packed panty hose. Once your boots are well sealed, try stomping through mud or walking through puddles. If you've done a good job of packing the needles and wrapping the tape, they should be warm and waterproof!

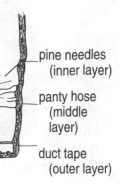

pine needles (inner layer)

panty hose (middle layer)

duct tape (outer layer)

❺ When you're ready to take off your boots, you can try to slip out of them, but you may need to cut your way out with the scissors. If so, make sure to get help from an adult.

 ANCIENT TREASURE MAP

What will you find buried in the place where *X* marks the spot? That is for you to decide when you create your own unique treasure map.

WHAT YOU'LL NEED

- permanent marking pens
- plain white paper
- 2 cups of strong coffee, cooled
- glass baking dish, 13 by 9 by 2 inches
- four paper towels, stacked
- 12-inch piece of ribbon, any color

DIRECTIONS

1 In the morning, ask an adult to save some coffee. You'll need at least a cup or two for this project.

2 Since most treasures are buried on islands, start your map by using permanent markers to draw an outline of an island on the paper.

3 Put a compass mark in one corner (showing which direction is north, south, east, and west). Draw in landmarks such as trees and cliffs. Add names of roads and mountains. Then mark a large *X* where the "treasure" is buried.

4 To make the map look ancient, you'll need to "age" the paper. Pour the cooled coffee into the baking dish. Put your map into the coffee bath and let it sit for thirty minutes. Remove the map and let the excess coffee drip into the baking dish. Lay the map on the paper towels.

5 When your map is wet, the paper can tear easily. Gently pull off bits of paper from the edges of the map to give it an uneven border. Then let the map dry. Once it's dry, carefully roll it up and tie the ribbon around it, then deliver it to a friend or family member with whom you want to share the secret of your treasure!

FURTHER FUN

Hide some real treasures, such as candy or a few coins, in your home or neighborhood. Then make a map showing where the treasure lies. Give the map to a friend to see if he or she can find the goodies.

THE AMAZING ART EXHIBIT

It's time for you and your friends to show off all the great artwork you've created over the years. Allow yourself at least one week to complete this project.

WHAT YOU'LL NEED

- one or more friends
- six or more pieces of artwork from each artist
- colored felt-tip pens
- 3-by-5-inch index cards
- construction paper

DIRECTIONS

DAY 1 *(at least one week before the show)*

1 Get a parent's permission to set up a temporary art show in a room of your home one day after school. (You'll also need to okay the exact date and time with them when you've decided upon it.)

2 Ask your friends if they'd like to help you put on an art exhibit. If they're interested, have each person bring his or her favorite pieces of artwork over to your house. You should have at least six pieces per artist—and more if there are only going to be two artists displaying their work. Artwork can include favorite paintings, clay statues, papier-mâché marvels . . . anything! If you don't have enough pieces, you can create some new art especially for the show. Once you have enough artwork collected, set a date for the exhibit. Store the art pieces somewhere out of reach of pets and younger siblings.

DAY 2 *(six days before the show)*

3 Make up a guest list of people you would like to invite, including parents, grandparents, brothers and sisters, friends, and neighbors.

4 Use colored pens and construction paper to make up invitations, which should tell what the event is, when it is, and where it is. Mail or hand deliver the invitations.

DAY 3 *(the day before the show)*

5 Take the pieces of art out of storage and arrange them around the room so guests who come for the viewing can see each piece well. They can be laid out on tables, set up on bookshelves, displayed on benches or chairs, or hung from the wall (if you have permission to use tape or tacks to put them up).

6 Your guests will want to know who made each piece, what the title of the piece is (if it has one), and the year it was created. Use 3-by-5-inch cards and the colored pens to make a label for each piece, then arrange the labels next to each piece of artwork.

7 Check the lighting in the room where you are going to have the show. If any of the art is placed in a dark area, set up a lamp or flashlight to shine on that piece, so guests will be sure to see it.

DAY 4 *(exhibit day!)*

8 Before the guests arrive, double check that all the artwork is in its proper place and labeled. Turn on any special lamps or lights. Then wait for the doorbell to ring.

9 Make sure all the artists are on hand to answer questions about their pieces. Help guide guests around the room so they're sure to see everything. Take a deep breath, and enjoy your time in the spotlight!

BELLS IN THE WIND

These beautiful ribboned bells are perfect for hanging outside a bedroom window or giving to a friend as an enchanting musical gift.

WHAT YOU'LL NEED

- twelve 10-inch strands of colored ribbon, $\frac{1}{8}$-inch wide or less (available at fabric stores)
- new unsharpened pencil
- white glue
- ten small jingle bells, about the size of cherries (available at art supply or craft stores)

DIRECTIONS

1 Tie a piece of ribbon to each end of the pencil, then tie the two ribbons together (see illustration). To secure, glue the ribbons in place on the pencil. Put aside.

2 While the glue is drying, take a new piece of ribbon and thread it through a bell. Tie it so that the bell hangs down from the end of the ribbon. Repeat for the remaining bells and ribbons.

3 Tie the free end of each ribbon around the pencil until all ten ribbons are tied to the pencil. Holding both ends of the pencil, raise it up and check whether all the bells are hanging at about the same level. If they aren't hanging at the same level, they won't knock together and make noise. Retie any ribbons to adjust the bells until they are all in a line. Slide the ribbons back and forth along the pencil to equally space out the bells, then glue all the ribbons in place on the pencil. Let it dry for thirty minutes.

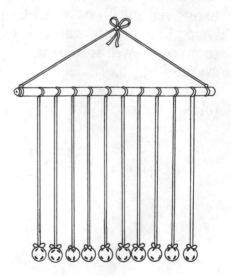

4 Take your wind chime outside, hang it from a hook or tree branch, and enjoy the music!

FIVE-TOE PICKUP

Are you good with your toes? Find out with this game that will challenge your podalic dexterity. (That's foot coordination, of course!)

WHAT YOU'LL NEED

- two players
- collection of buttons
- carpeted room
- two pie tins

DIRECTIONS

1 Take off your shoes and socks. The buttons are the game markers. Sprinkle the markers around the carpet (be sure to get permission first). Set the pie tins on opposite sides of the room. Each player "owns" one pie tin.

2 One person says "ready, set, go," and the players race to pick up the markers and put them into their own tin. Each player can only use his or her toes to pick up and move the markers. No hands! Players can pick up as many markers in one scoop as their toes can hold.

3 When all the markers have been gathered up, players count to see who has the most markers. That person is the winner!

FURTHER FUN

Try playing with more than two players. The more people that play, the wackier the game!

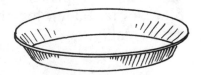

SUN SILHOUETTES

These sun silhouettes are a "bright" idea!

WHAT YOU'LL NEED

- sunny day
- sun printing paper (available at toy, hobby, or nature shops)
- small objects with distinctive outlines (such as leaves, keys, or jacks)
- shallow pan of water
- marking pens
- clear tape
- silver or gold glitter
- glue stick

DIRECTIONS

1 Gather all your materials first. The sun paper is light sensitive, so leave it in its packet until you need it.

2 Find a place outdoors that gets direct sunlight but is protected from the wind. Set down one sheet of sun paper. Use your shadow to shade the sun paper while you arrange your objects on it. Then step aside and leave the paper in the sun for five minutes.

3 Remove the objects and put the print into the pan of water. The water makes the silhouettes permanent. Lay the print in a safe, shaded place to dry. While your first print is drying, you can make another, and another, and another. Practice playing with different arrangements or using new objects to make your silhouettes.

4 Color the prints with marking pens, then use the glue stick and silver or gold glitter to decorate them.

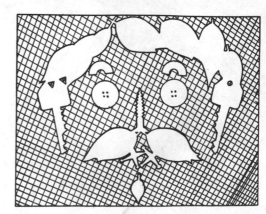

5 Hang your prints in your room, or tape a few together to wrap small gifts.

ADOBE ABODE

Mud, glorious mud! In this two-day project, recreate a miniature mud house.

WHAT YOU'LL NEED

- 6 cups dirt
- 4 cups water
- big bowl
- large mixing spoon
- 1 cup grass clippings

- four empty ice cube trays
- nonstick cooking spray
- shoe box lid
- pencil
- several long twigs

DIRECTIONS

DAY 1

1 Mix only 4 cups of dirt and 3 cups of water in the bowl until you have thick mud. The mixture should be able to drip in globs down the spoon, but not be runny. Stir in 1/2 cup of grass clippings and mix well.

2 Spray the inside of the ice cube trays with nonstick cooking spray. Fill the ice trays with the mud mixture and let it sit overnight in a warm, dry place.

DAY 2

3 After school, turn over the ice cube trays to remove the dried adobe bricks. Mix up the last 2 cups of dirt and cup of water to make a mud paste. Turn the shoe box lid facedown. Draw a rectangle about half the size of the box top inside the lid to show where the house walls will go.

4 Put down a layer of mud paste over the lines of the rectangle. Leave an open space at one end of the house for a door opening. Set a layer of bricks into the paste, then put down a layer of paste on top of this first layer of bricks. Continue building until you have four good-sized walls. Then set it aside to let the paste dry for thirty minutes.

5 Spread any remaining paste around the top of the house. Lay the twigs across the tops of opposite walls, sticking them into the wet paste. Fill in any holes in the roof with the extra grass clippings, then cover the roof with mud paste. Let dry overnight. You now have your own adobe abode!

TIME CAPSULE

Do you laugh at pictures of the clothing and hairstyles people wore years ago? Set up this time capsule, and you may be laughing at yourself in a couple of decades!

WHAT YOU'LL NEED

- recent magazines and newspapers
- movie ticket stub (with price)
- pictures of yourself, friends, and family
- shoe box with lid
- several sheets of plain white paper
- colored pens
- construction paper
- duct tape

DIRECTIONS

1 Gather up one or two copies of your favorite magazines, a current newspaper, a movie ticket stub, and a few current photos of yourself and your family (get a parent's permission first). Place these items in the shoe box, which will be your time capsule.

2 On the paper, write down lists of your favorite books, your school friends, and your favorite movies or TV shows. Stick them in the time capsule. Make a schedule of your typical day or week and add that to the time capsule, as well.

3 Have your best friend write a note to you, telling you about the activities he or she likes to do with you. Without reading it, put the note in the capsule.

4 Finally, with the construction paper and pens, make a small sign that says "This time capsule was created on . . ." and fill in the date, time, and year. Put the sign into the capsule. Close the capsule with its lid. Seal the time capsule securely by wrapping it over and over with duct tape.

5 Pick a date in the future—five or even ten years from now—when you will open it. (The longer you wait, the more fun you will have when you finally do open it.) On top of the time capsule, write in big bold letters "DO NOT OPEN UNTIL . . ." and write the date on which you want to open it. Then store it someplace where it won't get lost!

CAPTIVATING COUPONS

Coupon books are fun to create and make extra-special presents for those you love.

WHAT YOU'LL NEED

- notepad
- ballpoint pen
- ruler
- scissors
- construction paper
- colored pens
- hole punch
- yarn

DIRECTIONS

1 Think of all the people you depend on during the day—your mom or dad, an older brother or sister, even a good friend. You can make a book for one of these special people or make books for all of them.

2 With the notepad and pen, make a list of things you can do to help that person. For example, a big brother might appreciate having you do the dishes for him one night. Or a mother might love a few hours of baby-sitting.

3 Pick three or more activities from your list. Make one coupon for each activity. A good size for each coupon is $4\frac{1}{4}$ inches wide by $5\frac{1}{2}$ inches long. Measure and cut one piece of colored paper for each of your coupons.

4 On one of the pieces of construction paper, write "This coupon is good for . . ." and write in one of the favors. For example, "This coupon is good for taking out the trash any day of the week." Put only one activity on each coupon. Decorate each coupon as you wish.

5 Cut another piece of construction paper for the cover. Use the pens to decorate it. Include your name, the name of the person for whom you are making the book, and the occasion for which it's being given, if there is one. Arrange the coupons, with the cover on top. Using the hole punch, put two holes along the left side of the coupon book. Then cut two pieces of yarn in 8-inch lengths. Feed the first piece of yarn through the first hole, and tie it into a bow. Do the same with the second piece of yarn. Now it's ready to present. Once your coupon book is finished, don't forget to honor each and every coupon!

RADICAL ROCKET

Adventures in outer space await you aboard your own cosmic creation—
and it only takes two days to make!

WHAT YOU'LL NEED

- several sheets of newspaper
- cardboard tube from a roll of paper towels
- two paper towels
- scissors
- front and back cardboard panels from a cereal box
- white glue
- 1 cup liquid laundry starch
- shallow baking pan
- newspaper, cut into fifteen long, 2-inch-wide strips
- hobby paints and small paintbrushes
- ten strips of aluminum foil, each about $\frac{1}{8}$ inch wide by 5 inches long

DIRECTIONS

DAY 1

❶ Spread out newspaper to cover your work area.

❷ Set the cardboard tube, which will be the body of
your rocket, on the newspaper. Slightly dampen the
two paper towels, crumple them up together, and stuff
them halfway into one end of the tube. Mold the
remaining part of the damp towels into a pointed cone
for the nose of your rocket.

❸ Your rocket will need some
launching legs. Cut out three legs
from the cardboard cereal box panels. On the inside edge of each leg,
fold in a $\frac{1}{2}$-inch flap, which you will
then glue on to the rocket. Let them
dry for ten minutes.

4 Pour the liquid laundry starch into the shallow baking pan. One by one, take the newspaper strips and drag them through the liquid starch. Pull each wet newspaper strip through two of your fingers to remove any excess starch. Wrap the rocket in newspaper strips, making sure to cover all the parts so that the nose, body, and launching legs appear to be one unit. Let your rocket dry overnight.

DAY 2

5 Once your rocket is completely dry, paint it. You might want to put the name of a country on the side of the rocket, paint a country flag, or paint on windows with an astronaut peeking out.

6 During launch, a bright fuel fire usually burns from a rocket's engines. You can get this look of the sparkling fire by taking the strips of foil and gluing them to the bottom of the rocket. Now you're ready for takeoff!

SPOON MESSAGES

Before telephones or radios, people communicated over long distances using the sound signals of Morse code. You and a friend can use Morse code to send secret messages back and forth.

WHAT YOU'LL NEED

- two or more players
- two spoons per player
- paper
- pen or pencil

DIRECTIONS

1 Write down a copy of the Morse code for each player. Hold the spoons so that you can tap the backs of them together to make a loud clicking sound.

LETTERS:

A	.—
B	—...
C	—.—.
D	—..
E	.
F	..—.
G	——.
H	....
I	..
J	.———
K	—.—
L	.—..
M	——
N	—.
O	———
P	.——.
Q	——.—
R	.—.
S	...
T	—
U	..—
V	...—
W	.——
X	—..—
Y	—.——
Z	——..

2 In Morse code, every letter is represented by a series of short or long clicks. Timing is important, because the length of time between each click tells the listener whether he or she is hearing a short click or a long click. For example, to make the sound clicks for the letter *B*, click your spoons together once, pause, then click them together three times quickly. It's the pause that makes a click long.

3 To use the code, sit across a room from your friend. Ask "What word am I making?" then make the correct series of clicks. When you first play this game, the person making the clicks should pause after each letter to give enough time for the decoder to decode that letter. Once the decoder says "Okay!" then the person doing the clicking can move on to the next letter. (Once you get really good at hearing the letters, you won't need to stop after each letter. You can simply add long pauses between letters and extra-long pauses between words.)

4 When you've got the words down, it's time to send messages. At first, choose messages that are short. If you like this game and play it often, you may be able to create and understand messages without even having to look at your decoder list!

 # A WHALE OF A SECRET!

How do whales keep warm in icy seas? Try this experiment to discover every whale's secret!

WHAT YOU'LL NEED

• large bucket
• cold water
• two trays of ice
• pair of disposable plastic gloves
• spatula
• tub of lard or solid vegetable shortening
• kitchen timer

DIRECTIONS

1 Fill the bucket three-quarters full with cold water, then empty the ice from both ice trays into the bucket.

2 Put on the gloves. Use the spatula to completely cover one hand with lard or shortening. Leave the other gloved hand clean.

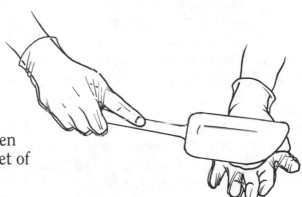

3 Use the clean hand to set a kitchen timer to five minutes, then plunge both hands into the bucket of ice water.

4 Watch the timer to find out how long you can keep each hand in the ice water. Don't let either hand get too cold before you pull it out!

5 How come one hand stayed so toasty warm? The lard or shortening acts just like a layer of whale blubber. It's pure fat and it helps keep the warmth in and the cold out. A layer of fat is the secret to how whales stay warm.

FAMOUS FOR A DAY

What is it like to be famous? Just imagine. . . .

WHAT YOU'LL NEED

- a friend
- a few sheets of 8½-by-11-inch paper, folded in half and stapled
- old magazines that you have permission to cut up
- pen • scissors • glue • colored pencils

DIRECTIONS

1 You and your friend are famous! Each of you decides whether you are a famous athlete, movie star, politician, chef, doctor, inventor, scientist, author . . . you can pick any profession you want.

2 Each of you makes a journal in which you'll keep notes about your day as a famous person (a few sheets of paper folded in half and stapled into a booklet will do). Imagine what one entire day would be like. Make a list in your journal of the specifics as you imagine them. What time do you need to get out of bed? What does your house look like? Do you and your friend get together to record music, practice a sport, or discuss new medical challenges? Write down as many details as you can about your lives as famous people.

3 Go through magazines and cut out at least five words or objects that would describe or show your lives as famous people. For example, a movie star might have special cars, expensive jewelry, or other luxuries. Glue the cutouts into your journal.

4 Using your list from Step 2 as a guide, reenact a few minutes of your famous life by spending a bit of time doing what you, as a famous person, do best. If you are a writer, write a story in your daily journal. If you are a rock star, turn on a rock radio station and do an impromptu performance for your friend. If you are a football star, reenact that 80-yard run (outside, please!) that won the game for your team.

MYSTERY MESSAGES

Surprise someone you care about with a special message from an "anonymous admirer"!

WHAT YOU'LL NEED

- pen or pencil
- scratch paper
- old magazines or newspapers that you have permission to cut up

- scissors
- glue
- construction paper

DIRECTIONS

1 Think of something nice you'd like to tell someone you care about. Do you think he or she gives the best hugs in the world? Does this person always take the time to listen to you? Decide what you would like to say and write it down in one or two sentences on the scratch paper.

2 Go through the magazines and newspapers and look for headlines and advertisements that contain the letters or words you need to create your note. Cut out and arrange the letters and words on a table so they spell out your message.

3 Glue the cutouts, in order, onto the construction paper, and let the glue dry. Fold your thoughtful message in half, and put it in a place where the recipient is sure to find it. Or you can drop it in the mail to the lucky person.

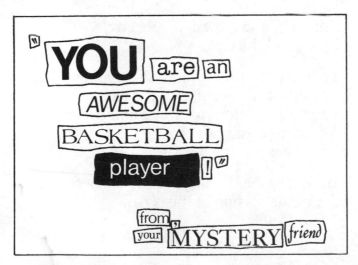

SPIRO-DESIGNS

Around and around and around it goes, the design will be made right under your nose!

WHAT YOU'LL NEED

- scissors
- string cut into 4-inch, 6-inch, and 8-inch pieces
- colored pens
- masking tape
- at least one 9-by-12-inch sheet of paper
- one 14-by-14-inch piece of stiff cardboard
- thumbtack

DIRECTIONS

1 Take the 4-inch piece of string and tie one end around one of the colored pens. Tie one end of the 6-inch piece of string around another colored pen. Then tie one end of the 8-inch piece of string to another pen.

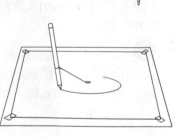

2 Place the paper onto the cardboard and tape down the corners.

3 Tie a knot in the loose end of one of the pieces of string. Put the tack through the knot, then push the tack into the middle of the paper. Hold the tack in place with one hand (to make sure it doesn't come loose) and pull the pen until the string straightens. Now keep the string tight and draw a perfect circle by moving the pen around the tack.

4 To move the pen into a new position, simply move the tack. Change the pens and the position of the tack until you have a beautiful geometric pattern of circles and curves (partial circles). For variety, you can change the lengths of the strings on the different colored pens.

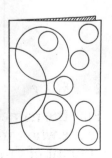

5 Fold your patterned paper in half and write a note to a friend on the plain, inside portion of the paper.

NAME GAME

You never know what could be hidden in your name. . . .

WHAT YOU'LL NEED

• colored pens
• 8½-by-11-inch piece of paper

DIRECTIONS

1 Write your name in big capital letters on the paper. Leave lots of room around each letter.

2 Look at your name as if you've never seen it before. Turn the paper sideways; look at it upside down. Examine closely the shape of each letter. With a little creativity, those letters could be transformed into extraordinary objects or animals. For example, if you have the letter *B* in your name, you can turn the *B* flat on its back and use the bumps to make the humps of a camel. The letter *D* could become a turtle or the back of a bus. What can you come up with? See how many objects and animals you can create using the letters of your name.

3 For a real challenge, choose a fun theme such as "at the amusement park" or "at the toy store." Then transform each of the letters of your name into items or objects related to your theme.

FURTHER FUN

Play the name game with a friend. Try trading names, or timing yourselves to see who can come up with the most creative ideas in the shortest amount of time.

 **DJ FOR A DAY**

It's time to rock and roll, hip and hop, or bring the classics home. It's your own radio show, where you pick the music and talk the talk that will bring your station to the top!

WHAT YOU'LL NEED

- radio
- pencil
- paper
- blank cassette tape
- tape recorder

DIRECTIONS

1 Decide what kind of radio station you want to create. Is it a classic rock, heavy metal, country, or classical music station? Turn on your radio to find a real station that plays the kind of music you've chosen, then turn down the volume while you create the outline for the script of your show.

2 Figure out what your radio personality name will be (you can use your real name or make up a funny name) and the name of the station. Write them down at the top of the paper.

3 No matter what kind of station you develop, there's bound to be a news broadcast between the songs you play. Think of current events at your school, in your community, or even in the world. You can even make up news events. List them on your sheet of paper.

4 If your radio show is like most others, you'll have to break for an advertisement from your sponsors. Think of a product you particularly like (or don't like) and make up a silly advertising jingle for it.

5 Use all the notes from above to write out an outline for your program. For example, your outline might look like this:
   a) a welcome (this is Wanda Witherspoon reporting)
   b) station identification (you're listening to KXYZ, 98.7 FM)
   c) identify the type of station (playing country morning, noon, and night)
   d) break for a song
   e) top news stories of the day

f) advertisement for the show's sponsor
g) break for another song
h) a sign-off (your name and station identification again)

6 Practice announcing all the parts of your show two or three times. When you're ready, record your broadcast on a blank cassette tape on the tape recorder. When it's time for a music break, turn up the real radio in the background to catch one of their songs or play a song from your personal music collection.

7 When you're finished recording, rewind the tape and listen to your show. If it's not quite right, you can start over until your show is just the way you want it.

8 Play your broadcast for your family after dinner.

FURTHER FUN

Arrange for an adult to take you and some friends on a tour of a *real* radio station. Maybe you can even interview someone at that station for your own radio program!

WINDSOCK WONDER

PARENTAL SUPERVISION RECOMMENDED
A breezy day is all you need to show off this colorful creation.

WHAT YOU'LL NEED

- scissors
- empty 18-ounce oatmeal container
- 9-by-14-inch piece of colored fabric
- white glue
- seven 12-by-2-inch pieces of colored fabric
- hole punch
- four pieces of string

DIRECTIONS

1 Use the scissors to cut the bottom out of the oatmeal container so that both ends are open—you may want to get a parent to help you with this step. Center the container on its side over the large piece of fabric. Line up the top of the container with the top edge of the fabric. An extra inch of the fabric should hang down below the bottom edge of the oatmeal container.

2 Wrap the sides of the fabric around the container and glue the fabric in place. The fabric should cover the entire container. Allow it to dry for at least twenty minutes.

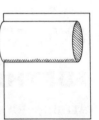

3 Take the extra inch of fabric that is hanging down from the bottom of the container and fold it inside the container, then glue it down. Glue the long fabric strips to the inside of the bottom of the container, so that they hang down like a skirt.

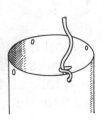

4 Use the hole punch to punch out four holes from the top of the oatmeal container. Tie a piece of string, about 10 inches long, through each hole, then tie all four pieces together, forming a knot at the top. Take the windsock outside and use the tied string to hang it from a branch or a hook on your front porch. Now watch the wind *sock* it around!

3/2 BLOOMING TERRARIUM

Create a small, living world and watch it grow!

WHAT YOU'LL NEED

- gravel
- large, wide-mouthed glass jar with lid
- granular-activated charcoal (available at garden shops)
- potting soil (available at garden shops)
- small plants, including any roots and a bit of the soil, gathered from outside (mosses, mushrooms, and ferns are good plants to try)
- rocks
- sticks or pieces of branch
- bottle opener

DIRECTIONS

1 Place ½ inch of the gravel in the bottom of the jar, followed by ½ inch of the charcoal. The gravel will keep excess moisture away from the plants. The charcoal will absorb acids that the plants give off as they grow. Without the charcoal, the terrarium's environment will become too acidic, and the plants will die.

2 Next, add about 3 inches of the potting soil and just enough water to make the soil damp. Carefully place the small plants in a pleasing arrangement in the jar, burying any roots into the soil.

3 Last, gently add a few pretty rocks and sticks to make the terrarium seem like a woodland scene. Screw on the jar's lid, and use the triangular end of a bottle opener to poke four holes in the lid for the plants to breathe. Place the terrarium in a sunlit room, but not in direct sunlight.

4 Terrarium plants don't need very much help to grow—just a little moisture, sunlight, and fresh air. Be careful not to overwater it—a few teaspoons of water each week should be enough. If the terrarium gets too wet, take off the lid for a few days and let the extra moisture evaporate.

LIQUID RAINBOW

Make a liquid rainbow right in your kitchen! It takes a slow and steady hand, but the results will look magical!

WHAT YOU'LL NEED

- newspapers
- measuring cup
- ¼ cup corn syrup
- food coloring (green, yellow, red, and blue)
- mixing spoon
- tall 8-ounce jar
- ¼ cup cold water
- measuring spoons
- 2 teaspoons salt
- teaspoon
- ¼ cup warm water
- ¼ cup rubbing alcohol

DIRECTIONS

1 Lay the newspapers out on a kitchen counter where you will be working. Fill the measuring cup with ¼ cup corn syrup. Add 2 drops of green food coloring and stir. Pour the green corn syrup into the jar. Try not to get any on the sides of the jar.

2 Wash the measuring cup thoroughly, then fill it with ¼ cup *cold* tap water. Add 2 teaspoons salt and stir until the salt is dissolved. Add 4 drops of yellow food coloring and stir.

3 This next step is very important. You need to pour the yellow saltwater into the jar in a way that keeps the corn syrup and the saltwater from mixing together. To do that, carefully lower a teaspoon into the jar until it hovers just above the green corn syrup. Put the spout of the measuring cup right up against the spoon handle, and slowly pour the saltwater down the handle of the spoon and into the jar. The saltwater should form a layer on top of the corn syrup.

4 Wash the measuring cup again and fill it with ¼ cup *warm* tap water. Add 4 drops of red food coloring and stir. Use the spoon technique mentioned in Step 3 to gently pour the red water into the jar. The red water should form a layer on top of the yellow saltwater.

5 Wash the cup again, then measure ¼ cup rubbing alcohol. Add 2 drops of blue food coloring and stir. Use the spoon technique to pour the blue rubbing alcohol into the jar. The rubbing alcohol will partially mix wih the red water and also form a layer on top.

6 Step back and admire your rainbow!

WARNING: Do *not* swallow this mixture or leave it unattended where someone might mistake it for a drink. The rubbing alcohol and saltwater can make a person extremely ill if swallowed.

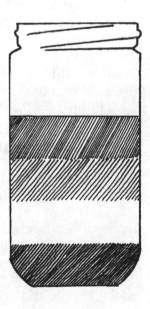

34 STAINED "GLASS" MOBILE

These creative circles capture the colors of the rainbow and bring them right into your home!

WHAT YOU'LL NEED

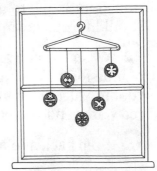

- lid to peanut butter or mayonnaise jar
- black construction paper
- colored cellophane wrap in at least three colors
- nylon fishing line, cut in 5-, 7-, 9-, 11-, and 13-inch pieces
- pencil
- scissors
- glue
- glitter
- wire hanger

DIRECTIONS

1 Place the jar lid on the construction paper and trace ten circles. Cut out each circle. You'll need two circles for each "window" that will hang from your mobile.

2 Take two of the circles and stack them one atop the other. Now fold the two circles in half and begin cutting squares, triangles, or any other shape from the *creased* side of the circle. You can cut the circles any way you'd like, but be sure to leave the outside edge of the circles intact.

3 Unfold the circles to see the pattern you've made. Place the two circles down on a table, and move the top circle aside. Cut a piece of colored cellophane for the open space in your pattern. Make the cellophane slightly larger than the open space, and glue it in place. Then glue one of the pieces of the fishing line to the top of the pattern.

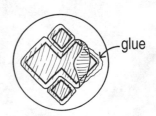
glue

4 Take the black cut-out circle that you set aside and glue it onto the circle with the cellophane, aligning cut-out sections. Allow the glue to dry.

5 Repeat Steps 2, 3, and 4 until you've created five windows. Decorate the edge of each small window by gluing on some glitter.

6 Tie the loose end of each piece of fishing line onto the hanger, fasten it in front of a window or another well-lit spot, and enjoy the rainbow of colors!

CREATE A CRITTER

A strange spirit creature from outer space has become stranded on Earth and needs your help. Can you give it a body to live in, a nice nest to sleep in, and a place to call home?

WHAT YOU'LL NEED

- old tennis ball
- pipe cleaners
- empty spools of thread
- construction paper
- clay
- scissors

- glue
- dryer lint
- small, empty cardboard box (such as a tissue box)
- colored pens
- white 3-by-5-inch index card

DIRECTIONS

1 Decide what kind of body to give your critter. The tennis ball makes a good starting point. Use such objects as pipe cleaners, spools of thread, construction paper, and clay to add legs, wings, antennae, eyes, or anything else you think your critter needs as part of its body. Shape these materials into your critter's body parts. Attach them to the body using glue where needed.

2 Make a nest for your critter by putting lint gathered from the clothes dryer in the empty cardboard box. Decorate the box with colored pens and write your critter's name on the outside of it.

3 Because this critter is from outer space, it may feel very misunderstood here on Earth. Write a description of your animal on the 3-by-5-inch card. Tell how it got here, what and how it eats, and what its own planet is like. Place the note card inside your animal's nest.

4 Show off your alien critter to your friends and family. And be sure to take good care of it. After all, it's depending on you!

THE ZOTZ CAME IN A ROCKET FROM ZOTO-A PLANET COVERED BY RAINFOREST. IT LIKES TO EAT BUGS ESPECIALLY FROM OUR GARDEN!

ZOTZ

 # FOAM GLIDER PLANE

It sails through the air with the greatest of ease, and you probably won't get in trouble for flying it in the house!

WHAT YOU'LL NEED

- scissors
- foam egg carton
- pencil
- ruler
- ballpoint pen
- two or three paper clips

DIRECTIONS

1 Cut out the flat, top panel of an egg carton. Use a pencil to copy the pattern of the three plane pieces pictured on the next page onto the carton. Use the ruler to make sure that the large wing is 1 inch wide and the small wing is ¾ inch wide. Cut out each piece.

2 Use a ballpoint pen to mark the two slits on the body of the plane. The slit near the front of the plane should be 1 inch long and angle upward very slightly. The slit near the tail should be ¾ inch long. Press hard with the tip of the pen to gouge out the slits in the plane.

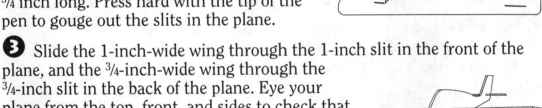

3 Slide the 1-inch-wide wing through the 1-inch slit in the front of the plane, and the ¾-inch-wide wing through the ¾-inch slit in the back of the plane. Eye your plane from the top, front, and sides to check that the wings are placed evenly from side to side.

4 Toss your plane in the air for a test flight. The main wing can be adjusted up if the plane goes down nose-first, or down if the plane flies upward too sharply. To make the adjustment, pull out the main 1-inch wing and use the tip of the pen to gouge out a new angle (that is, make the slit angle higher or lower) in the front slit. As long as you don't change the 1-inch *width* of the slit, the wing will stay in place even with a slight space above or below the wing. You can also try adding a paper clip or two to the body (anywhere between the wings) to change the flight patterns of your plane.

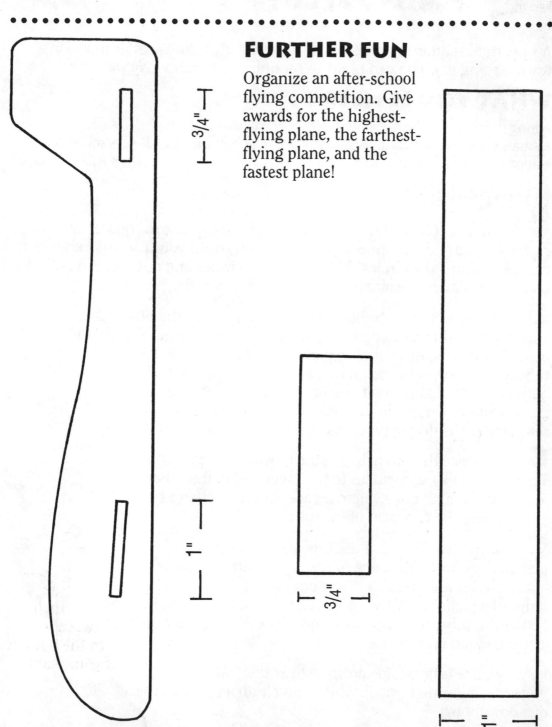

FURTHER FUN

Organize an after-school flying competition. Give awards for the highest-flying plane, the farthest-flying plane, and the fastest plane!

3/4"

1"

3/4"

1"

THE SUNNY DAY RAIN STICK

A rain stick is an instrument used in some African musical groups. On a warm spring day, you can use it to remind you of rainy-day weather!

WHAT YOU'LL NEED

- long cardboard tube (an empty gift-wrap roll works well)
- small square of flat cardboard (such as cereal box cardboard)
- approximately 2 cups of split peas
- pen
- scissors
- masking tape

DIRECTIONS

1 Stand the tube up on its end on top of the cardboard square. Trace a circle around the bottom of the tube. Repeat, until you have made seven circles. Cut out the circles. Take five of the circles and cut them in half to create ten semicircles; leave two of the circles whole.

2 Cut the tube in a straight line from one end to the other. Then make another straight cut along the opposite side of the tube. You should be left with two gutter-shaped pieces of tube. Take one half of the tube and fit one of the semicircles inside the tube. Tape it on both sides, so that it won't flap back and forth when the peas run up and down inside your rain stick. Tape four more semicircles inside the tube, spacing them equally apart.

3 Now place the two halves of the tube next to each other. Tape the last five semicircles to the other half of the tube. Make sure that all ten semicircles are placed at different points along the two sides of the tube.

4 Put the two halves of the tube back together and tape securely. Take one of the whole cardboard circles and use it to cover one end of the long tube. Tape the circle in place. Pour the peas into the open end of the tube, then cover the open end with the last cardboard circle and tape it in place.

5 Turn the tube upside down to hear the "rain." A slow turn gives you a gentle rainfall, while a quick turn imitates the sound of a downpour!

FURRY FRIEND

PARENTAL SUPERVISION REQUIRED
These fuzzy critters are a ball of fun to make!

WHAT YOU'LL NEED

- two pieces of thick cardboard, 5-by-5-inches square
- scissors
- small ball of yarn, any color
- 12-inch piece of yarn, cut from the ball
- black and white construction paper
- white glue

DIRECTIONS

❶ Place the two squares of cardboard together and cut them into matching circles. Have an adult help you use the scissors to carefully poke a hole in the middle of the circles and cut out an inner circle. When you're finished cutting, the two pieces of cardboard should look like doughnuts. The hole in the middle should be big enough for the ball of yarn to pass through.

❷ Thread the end of the ball of yarn through the cutout hole of *both* cardboard pieces and tie it securely. Now begin wrapping the yarn through the hole, around the cardboard, then back through the hole. Repeat this until the hole in the cardboard is completely filled with yarn.

❸ Use the scissors to snip the yarn along the entire rim of the "doughnut." The cut yarn will fall away from the rim, exposing the two cardboard pieces. Gently pull the two cardboard pieces apart until there is a slight gap between them. If you pull the two pieces all the way off the yarn, the yarn will fall into a heap at your feet. To keep the bunch of yarn together, take the 12-inch piece of yarn and slide it between the two cardboard pieces, then tie it in a tight knot around the yarn pieces. When the knot is secure, slowly pull the two pieces of cardboard off the yarn. Fluff the yarn ball.

❹ Cut the construction paper to make eyes, then glue them onto your fuzzy friend. Make large and small fuzzies using different sizes of cardboard doughnuts.

RECYCLED PAPER

Making recycled paper is an excellent way to turn junk mail into something exotic and expressive.

WHAT YOU'LL NEED

- newspaper
- two large bowls or buckets
- warm water
- blender
- clothes dryer lint
- food coloring
- shallow, recycled tin can (such as a tuna can)
- can opener
- cheesecloth (a fine meshed cloth available at grocery stores)
- rubber band
- four old dishcloths
- dry sponge
- rolling pin
- heavy books

DIRECTIONS

1 Tear the newspaper into 1-inch squares. Fill one of the large bowls with warm water. Put the squares into the bowl and soak for at least half an hour.

2 Pour 2 cups of fresh warm water into your blender, then add a handful of the wet newspaper and a cotton-ball-sized bundle of lint from the dryer. Blend until it forms a thin, bubbly liquid. If the mixture seems too thick, add a little water. Put a few drops of food coloring (any color will work) into the blender and blend again. For darker colors, add more food coloring.

3 The tin can you've recycled should be empty and clean. Use the can opener to remove the remaining lid, so that the can is open from both ends. The shape of the can will determine the shape of your paper—a round can will give you round paper; a square can will give you square paper.

4 Cover one side of the can with cheesecloth. Hold the cheesecloth in place with the rubber band. Pour ½ inch of clear water into the remaining clean bowl. Place the cheesecloth-covered can into the bowl, cloth-side down, letting it sit in the water.

5 Pour 1 cup of the paper mixture into the can, then swish it around. Lift the can out of the bowl. Let the excess water drip back into the bowl. Then place the can on a dishcloth and let it drain for about ten minutes.

6 Move the can to a new, dry place on the dish-cloth. Remove the rubber band, and carefully lift the tin away from the paper mixture. Press the flat paper cake with the dry sponge to remove excess liquid. When the paper cake is dry enough, you should be able to pick it up, turn it over, and peel the cheese-cloth away.

7 Cover the sheet of paper with another dishcloth and roll it with the rolling pin to squeeze out any remaining moisture. Place it on another dry dish-cloth. Now go back to Step 4. Keep making paper cakes until all the paper mixture is gone. Cover the paper cakes with one last dishcloth, then stack two or three heavy books on top of the dish-cloth. Your paper should be completely dry and ready to use in twenty-four hours.

40 SHIMMERY SHOELACES 1

Fancy feet are only a few fun steps away!

WHAT YOU'LL NEED

- newspaper
- two pairs of white shoelaces
- colored permanent markers
- white glue
- glitter

DIRECTIONS

1 Spread the newspaper over your work area and lay out your shoelaces, markers, glue, and glitter.

2 Use the marking pens to color both sides of each lace. You can use one or many colors for each lace—let your imagination go wild! To make rainbow-colored shoelaces, color sections of red, orange, yellow, green, and blue.

3 After the shoelaces have been colored, it's time to add some sparkle. Hold the tip of the glue bottle as if it were a pencil. Then draw a glue design on the shoelaces. Sprinkle the glitter onto the shoelaces wherever you have put glue. Let the glue and glitter dry for thirty to sixty minutes.

4 Now you're ready to replace those plain laces on your shoes with these flashy, colorful creations!

KRAZY KOUNTRY

 **1**

Will you be the King of Krakatoa? The Great Sheba of Shozbotland? The President of Preladonia? You decide when you discover your own new country.

WHAT YOU'LL NEED

- colored pens
- colored construction paper
- scissors
- white glue

DIRECTIONS

1 Imagine you are an explorer. You come upon an undiscovered island with gold mines and no inhabitants. You can spend all the money you want to create whatever country you wish. What do you do?

2 Start by thinking of a name for your country. The name can be silly or serious, depending on your mood and the kind of image you want your country to have. Write the name at the top of a piece of light-colored construction paper.

3 Next, use the colored construction paper, scissors, and colored pens to make the flag. Almost all the flags that represent nations of the world are rectangular. But that doesn't mean that yours can't be circular, triangular, star-shaped, or whatever shape you want.

4 Now decide on the ten laws that are most important to your country. What is legal and illegal? Will children get big allowances paid for by the government? Write down all your laws on a separate sheet of construction paper. These laws will make up your Kountry Konstitution!

5 Draw a map of your country on a sheet of construction paper. Where are the borders? Will there be amusement parks, movie theaters, and jungle gyms?

6 When you are done, hang everything on a bulletin board or on your wall to display your new country.

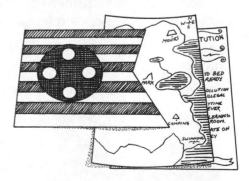

 # OUR FAMILY BOARD GAME

So you're in charge of entertainment for the evening's festivities? Turn off the tube, and put together a game your family will never forget!

WHAT YOU'LL NEED

- at least one family member
- ruler
- colored pens
- 2-by-2-foot cardboard square
- pencil
- paper
- scissors
- dice

- family photos that can be cut up (get permission first!)
- white glue
- strips of thin cardboard (made from the side of a cereal box)
- 5-inch-wide square of foil for each game marker

DIRECTIONS

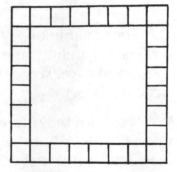

❶ Use the ruler and pens to mark your cardboard so that each side has eight equal sections (see illustration). Choose one corner to be the home base, then color and decorate it.

❷ Next, you'll need to write four lists. The first list should be a list of birthdays for seven members of your family. The second list should be a list of seven homes of relatives or close friends you visit often (for example, Grandma's house). The third list should be a list of seven special holidays that are meaningful to your family (for example, Thanksgiving or Cinco de Mayo). The last list should be a list of *six* favorite family stories that begin with "Remember the time when . . ." For example, "Remember the time when Kelly made a joke while Tim was drinking grape juice and he started to laugh and it all came out his nose?"

❸ Write one item from your lists in each square on your board game. Mix up the items so that the birthdays, homes, and events are sprinkled around the board. Decorate your board with colored pens.

4 To make the game markers, carefully cut out each family member from a family photo (remember to get permission!). You'll need at least two game markers, but it's better to have one for every member of the household. Glue a strip of the thin cardboard along the back of each photo to keep it stiff, then scrunch a piece of foil around the bottom of each photo to make a stand.

5 Now you're ready to play. Choose which family member you want to "play." That person's cutout photo will be your marker. Pick carefully because, for the rest of the game, you'll need to talk in that person's voice, say the types of things he or she would say, and use his or her gestures.

6 To see who goes first, each player rolls the dice. The high roller goes first, the player on his or her left goes second, and so on. The first player starts at home base, rolls the dice, then moves his or her marker the number of spaces that are on the dice. In the voice and characteristics of the family member that he or she is "playing," the player must say or do something that that person would do at the event, situation, or place written on the square. For example, if you are using the "Dad" marker and you land on the square marked "Thanksgiving," you might begin snoring if your father is known to fall asleep after a big meal.

If you land on someone's birthday, you get an extra turn. Any player who makes a rude comment or puts down a family member loses a turn.

7 Take turns traveling around the board. The first player to go around the board three times is the winner!

67

43 THROUGH WIZENED EYES

Imagine you are eighty years old, and you've decided to write a book about your life. What will you say?

WHAT YOU'LL NEED

- pen
- paper
- folder

DIRECTIONS

1 A book written about one's own life is called an autobiography. Most of the time, autobiographies are written by famous people, such as politicians, actors, and sports stars. Here, you'll use your imagination to journey into the future and see yourself as an old person who has had an exciting and influential life. From the perspective of your older, wiser self, write about what your life "was" like.

2 Make a list of the milestones or great things that you accomplished in your life. Did you go to college, travel the world, raise a family? Make sure you think of at least one big event to put down for every decade of your life. If you're having trouble figuring out what someone in each stage of life might be doing, ask your grandparents, parents, or some older friends.

3 Imagine your one greatest accomplishment. Write it down in detail. If you were a paleontologist, don't just write down that you found some dinosaur bones. What type of dinosaur bones were they? What did newspapers or magazines write about your discovery?

4 Now use your list of milestones and greatest accomplishments to write your autobiography. Keep the pages of your autobiography tucked neatly in the folder. Decorate your folder as you wish.

5 Store your autobiography in a safe, hidden place for the years to come. You may decide to read it again when you're twenty or thirty to see which milestones in your life you've already passed!

FURTHER FUN

This is an excellent activity to do every year or so. As you get older, you'll find you have different priorities and new goals to fit your changing life.

 # A FEAST FOR THE BIRDS

The feathery fliers in your neighborhood will love these tasty treats.

WHAT YOU'LL NEED

- dinner knife
- 1 cup peanut butter
- four small apples with stems
- 2 cups birdseed (available at grocery or pet stores)
- small pan
- plate

DIRECTIONS

1 Use the dinner knife to spread peanut butter all over each apple (except for the stem).

2 Pour the birdseed into the small pan.

3 Roll the apples around in the birdseed. The birdseed will stick to the peanut butter. Keep rolling the apples until all the peanut butter is completely covered by birdseed. Place the finished apples on a plate.

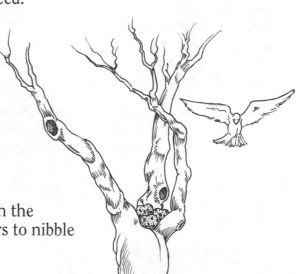

4 Take the plate outside. Find a tree with strong, low branches. Place the apples in the crooks of the tree—where the tree trunk meets a branch. Make sure the apples are steady so that when a bird comes along to peck at them, the apples won't fall out of the tree.

5 Go back into the house and watch the tree from a window to see who appears to nibble the delightful delicacies you've left.

MAGNETIC ICE RINK

Create a "magic" magnetic skater that seems to whirl and twirl on the ice all by itself.

WHAT YOU'LL NEED

- scissors
- large cardboard cereal box
- aluminum foil
- clear tape

- pencil
- tracing paper
- heavy construction paper
- scissors

- colored pens
- glue
- glitter
- two paper clips
- 1-inch magnet

DIRECTIONS

1 Cut out the front panel of the cereal box, then tear off a piece of foil that is a little larger than the cereal box panel. Cover one side of the panel with foil. Keep the foil in place by taping down the edges on the underside of the panel. This is your ice rink.

2 Trace the pattern of the ice skater (see illustration on the next page) onto a piece of tracing paper, and cut it out with the scissors. Make sure not to cut off the tab on the bottom. Using the tracing paper figure as an outline, trace the skater onto a piece of heavy construction paper and cut it out. With the colored pens, draw a face and ice-skating clothes on *both* sides of the paper skater. Glue glitter onto the skater's outfit.

3 Glue two paper clips to the tab (see illustration), then fold the tab so that the ice skater "stands" upright. Place the ice skater on the "ice," then hold the magnet underneath the ice rink. The magnet will attract the paper clips at the base of the skater. Wherever you move the magnet, the skater will appear to "skate" on the rink.

— magnet

4 Practice making different skating moves with your skater. Turn the magnet quickly to make the skater appear to spin, or try making the skater glide in a figure-eight pattern around the rink.

FURTHER FUN

Make a second skater and see if you can move the two skaters around the rink as a coordinated pair. Or have a friend make a skater, add on Popsicle® stick hockey sticks, and play a game of one-on-one hockey using a small, crumpled piece of paper as the puck.

← tab

46 FAMILY FRIDGE FACES

Have an important note to put on your refrigerator? Use these fun—and goofy—homemade magnets that look like the people in your family.

WHAT YOU'LL NEED

- mixing bowl
- ½ cup flour
- ¼ cup salt
- ¼ cup water
- mixing spoon
- teaspoon
- cutting board

- foil-covered cookie sheet
- garlic press
- white glue
- ten flat, round magnets, about the size of a quarter (available at hardware stores or art supply stores)
- acrylic paints and thin paintbrushes

DIRECTIONS

1 In the bowl, combine the flour, salt, and water. Stir with the mixing spoon until the mixture becomes thick, then pick it up with your hands and squish it together until you have a smooth dough.

2 Scoop out 1 teaspoonful of dough and place it on the cutting board. Roll the dough into a ball, then squash it into a circle. Make six circles. Each round shape should be about ¼-inch thick and a little larger than a quarter. Place each circle onto the foil-covered cookie sheet.

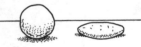

3 Using the leftover dough, decorate each circle with the features of a family member. Roll tiny dough eyes and shape tiny mouths, then put them in place. To make hair, press some of the dough through the garlic press. Imitate each person's hairstyle to make the faces easier to identify.

4 Place the cookie sheet into the freezer until the faces are firm, about one hour.

5 Next, turn each face over and glue on a magnet, then turn it faceup again. Paint the faces, including the eyes, mouths, and hair. Let the magnets dry overnight, then display them on the fridge for all to see!

47 THE AFTER-SCHOOL CLUB

Start a club that anyone can join and organize projects for your whole neighborhood to enjoy.

WHAT YOU'LL NEED

- two or more friends
- meeting place

DIRECTIONS

1 Think of the friends whom you'd like to have join your club. Pick the people you like to spend time with, but try not to exclude people whose feelings might be hurt if they were left out. Decide on a good place to meet. The meeting place could be one member's room, a corner of a family room, or outside in a favorite shed or under a tree.

2 Consider the talents and favorite hobbies of all the members and come up with a name that could only apply to your group of friends. Invent a unique handshake so you can greet each other in a special way when you're together as a club.

3 Write up your club's "constitution." It can include such things as your club name, the members' names, a description of the secret handshake, your club mascot, and the purpose of the club.

4 One good way to work together as a club is to have a homework/study session first thing after school. All the club members can help each other out, with members sharing their special academic talents with each other. When you're done, your club can organize neighborhood-wide games for *all* the kids to play.

73

CLUB COOKIE BAKE

Here's a special two-day activity for your After-School Club that's fun for you and a super way to light up someone's day.

WHAT YOU'LL NEED

- at least three club members
- address and phone number of a local nursing home or children's hospital
- a favorite cookie recipe from each member (and cookie ingredients)
- mixing bowls, wooden spoons, and cookie sheets
- box of plastic sandwich bags
- at least fifty ribbons

DIRECTIONS

DAY 1 *(making the cookies)*

1 Find out if one of your parents would be willing to drive you and your friends on a special delivery errand the next day. Once you find a driver, call up a local nursing home or children's hospital and find out if it would be okay for you to deliver home-baked cookies for the residents or patients the next day. Find out how many residents there are (if there are more than fifty, you may need to find a smaller home or hospital, unless you want to bake lots of cookies). Once you've gotten an official okay, you're ready to go!

2 Multiply the number of residents or patients by two (so that you can deliver at least two cookies to each person). For example, if a nursing home has twenty-five residents, you'd need to make at least fifty cookies.

3 When you've figured out how many cookies you'll need to bake, collect recipes from your club members, and make as many varieties as you want. Gather all the ingredients at one person's house, and follow the recipes as you mix up a storm! (Remember to make a few extras for your families, too.)

4 Let the cookies cool for at least one hour, then put at least two cookies in each sandwich bag. Tie a bow around each bag. Make sure you have enough bags for each resident or patient. Store the cookies in a safe place overnight.

DAY 2 *(delivering the cookies)*

5 The next day after school, gather everyone together, put the cookies in the car, and head off to the nursing home or children's hospital. Meet the person with whom you spoke on the phone, and tell him or her that you are here to make your special delivery. Hand out the cookies to each resident or patient. Some of the people whom you meet might be very eager to talk to someone. Take a moment to say hello—it could be the best thing that happens to that person all day.

6 When you're done passing out your treats, congratulate each other on a job well done. You've brought smiles and happiness to many people!

 **SILLY SIGNS**

You and a friend can develop your own silent, silly language; no one else will know what you're talking about!

WHAT YOU'LL NEED

• a friend

DIRECTIONS

1 Baseball coaches tell their players on base and at bat what to do by using secret hand signals. Deaf people communicate using hand gestures called sign language. You and your friends can communicate in the same silent way by making up your own hand signals.

2 Start by thinking of a few sentences you and your friend say to each other often. Examples include:
"Let's go over to my house."
"I aced my test!"
"That guy/girl is really cute!"

3 For each sentence, you'll need to come up with a silent signal equivalent. You can use any combination of hand, leg, arm, or head movements, including tapping your feet, crossing your fingers, bobbing your head, or touching your ear in a particular way. If the movements are big, people will know you're up to something. If they are small and subtle, others may not know there's something going on.

4 Practice using your signs until you and your friend can make the signs quickly and read them easily. Test each other when you are by yourselves. When you've got them memorized, try them out silently in front of others.

FURTHER FUN

You can gradually build a whole repertoire of signs and signals. You and your friend can set a goal to learn a new signal a week, or three new signals a week—whatever you decide.

 **MUNCHABLE MOON ROCKS**

Munch, munch, crunch, crunch. Moon rocks look a little odd, but the taste is out of this world.

WHAT YOU'LL NEED

- 1 cup peanut butter (chunky or smooth)
- 1½ cups marshmallow creme
- large mixing bowl
- mixing spoon
- 1 cup semisweet chocolate chips
- 1 cup crispy rice cereal
- tablespoon
- ungreased cookie sheet
- plastic sandwich bags (one for each member of your family)
- note cards
- pen

DIRECTIONS

1 Combine the peanut butter and marshmallow creme in the bowl. Stir with the spoon until they are thoroughly mixed.

2 Add the chocolate chips. The mixture will be fairly thick and hard to stir, so use your muscles!

3 Add the crispy rice cereal. Stir just long enough to mix in the cereal without crushing it into a fine powder.

4 Take a heaping tablespoonful of the mixture and roll it into a ball. Place the ball on the ungreased cookie sheet. Keep making balls until all the mixture is used up. Place the cookie sheet in the refrigerator and chill for at least two hours.

5 Count out one sandwich bag for each member of your family. Place two or three moon rocks in each bag. Secretly place one bag on each person's pillow with a note saying "Sweet Dreams!"

THE PERFECT PROJECT FOR THE PERFECT OCCASION

Choosing an activity is easy with this quick-reference list. Just select a category and find an activity that interests you. Many of the projects listed here overlap.

ON YOUR OWN

GIFTS FOR SOMEONE SPECIAL

Use your free time after school to make a gift for a friend or a family member. No matter what the occasion, you can create a thoughtful present for someone you care about. These are some of the projects that can easily be turned into a cool gift:

To Do with a Friend or Two

When the Whole Crew Is Together

Just for the Outdoors

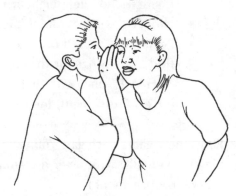

Parental Supervision Recommended or Required

Activities that Take More than One Day

Extra-Easy Projects

Tournament of Fun

Turn after-school fun into a week-long event with a "Tournament of Fun." As the organizer you will need to:

- invite friends and neighborhood kids to participate
- choose the games and put together a point system
- keep track of each day's points for every team
- find a cool prize for the champion (Be creative—find a rock and paint "CHAMP" on it with that person's initials and the date. Then each time you have a tournament, the rock can be passed from winner to winner.)

Play a new game each day. You can play in rounds if you need to. Choose teams or play individually, whichever the group prefers. Here are a few activities that are great for tournament fun: